WINSTON CHURCHILL

Simon Adams

W
FRANKLIN WATTS
LONDON•SYDNEY

Maps Ian Thompson
Designer Stuart Packard
Editor Penny Clarke
Art Director Jonathan Hair
Editor-in-Chief John C. Miles

Consultant Eileen Yeo, Professor of
Social and Cultural History, University
of Strathclyde

This edition 2006

First published in 2003
by Franklin Watts
338 Euston Road
London
NW1 3BH

Franklin Watts Australia
Hachette Children's Books
Level 17/207 Kent Street
Sydney NSW 2000

© 2003 Franklin Watts

ISBN 0 7496 6719 2

A CIP catalogue record
for this book is available
from the British Library.

Printed in China

Dewey classification: 941.082'092

Picture credits
Front cover: Topham Picturepoint
(main and background)
p 2 Topham Picturepoint
p 3 Topham Picturepoint
AKG London pp 25, 27, 31, 32, 36,
69, 81
Hulton Archive pp 32, 47, 49
Sue Mennell p 95
Peter Newark's Military Pictures pp 5,
8, 15, 19, 23, 57, 71, 79, 85, 101
Popperfoto pp 7, 9, 10, 13, 17, 21,
29, 34, 39, 41, 44, 51, 52, 58, 61, 63,
66, 84, 89, 91, 92, 96, 97
Topham Picturepoint pp 43, 53, 55,
64, 73 (Associated Press), 74, 77, 98

Winston Churchill
1874–1965

Contents

Introduction

Extraordinary events bring forward extraordinary people. In 1940, when Britain stood almost alone against the might of Nazi Germany, one man stepped forward to lead his nation. His name was Winston Churchill.

Winston Churchill was born in Oxfordshire, England, on 30 November 1874 and died in London on 24 January 1965 aged 90. Although born in a palace, he did not have a particularly privileged or happy child-hood and his education was poor. As a politician he often made mistakes; yet he still dominated British politics for most of the 20th century.

In this biography we follow Churchill's career through the army and into politics as a Member of Parliament in 1900. We look at why he changed parties in 1904 and see how he rose to high office before resigning in disgrace in 1915. We follow his return to power in 1917 and his second change of political parties in the 1920s before, in the 1930s, he consigned himself to the political wilderness again. None of this, however, stopped him achieving the ultimate political prize: in 1940, at the age of 65, he became prime minister in the darkest days of World War Two. Defeat seemed almost inevitable, but through his leadership he led his nation to victory.

Behind the political figure was a complex and fascinating man. He inspired great loyalty from his supporters and friends, yet many people thought he was unreliable and distrusted his views. But he gave the country what it needed during the war. Outside politics he was a good painter and an excellent writer – he won the Nobel Prize for Literature in 1953 – and even prided himself on his skill as bricklayer! But he lived for politics. Controversial during his life, his reputation remains assured as one of the great leaders of the 20th century, whose contribution really did change the history of the world.

▶ *A photograph of Winston Churchill taken near the end of World War Two in 1945.*

Early life

Winston Churchill was born in a splendid palace, into a family who were part of the British aristocracy.

Blenheim Palace is a vast country house set in beautiful parkland outside the small town of Woodstock, near Oxford in southern England. The palace, built between 1705–22, was a gift from Queen Anne of England to John Churchill, 1st Duke of Marlborough. It was a thank-you for his military skill, especially his defeat of the French army of Louis XIV at the battle of Blenheim in southern Germany in 1704. The palace was designed by Sir John Vanbrugh, the leading architect of the time, and is full of exquisite paintings, wood carvings, sculptures and furniture.

Churchill's parents

On 30 November 1874 Winston Leonard Spencer Churchill was born at Blenheim. His father was Lord Randolph Churchill, third son of the 7th Duke of Marlborough. Because Randolph was the son of a duke he had the courtesy title of "Lord", but as he was not the eldest son he could not sit in the House of Lords.

In February 1874 Randolph was elected to the House of Commons as Conservative Member of Parliament (MP) for the Woodstock constituency. He was a brilliant public speaker, but many MPs distrusted him, seeing him as an opportunist with few political principles. In 1885 he became Secretary of State for India, and then, in 1886, Chancellor of the Exchequer. However, he soon fell out with the prime minister, Lord Salisbury, and resigned in December 1886. He never held office again and died a political failure in January 1895.

Churchill's mother, Jennie Jerome, was born in Brooklyn, New York. She was the daughter of Leonard Jerome, a New York financier and briefly part-owner of the *New York Times* newspaper. Jerome was a horse-racing enthusiast and founded the Jerome Park race track and the Coney Island Jockey Club. The Duke of

▶ *Lord Randolph Churchill, Winston Churchill's father, became MP for Woodstock, Oxfordshire, in 1874. Like his son he was a brilliant public speaker.*

▲ *Winston Churchill (right) photographed with his mother, Jennie Jerome, and younger brother Jack in 1889.*

Marlborough did not consider that the daughter of an American financier was a suitable match for his aristocratic son. Jennie, however, was a beautiful young woman – some of her good looks came from her Iroquois Native American grandmother. Jennie had spent much of her childhood in Paris and was at first very much in love with her husband. However, she later had numerous romantic affairs and there has always been speculation that her second child,

Jack, born in Dublin, Ireland, in 1880, was not Randolph's son.

After Randolph's death in 1895, she married twice more. Both marriages were to younger men, the first of whom, George Cornwallis-West, was only two weeks older than Winston. They divorced in 1914. Jennie then married Montagu Porch in 1917.

Education in late 19th-century Britain

When Churchill was a child, at the end of the 19th century, the sons of rich parents were first taught by a nanny or governess at home before attending a fee-paying preparatory school, such as the ones at Ascot and Brighton where Churchill was sent. At about 12 or 13 boys sat entrance examinations for one of Britain's many famous public schools, such as Harrow, where Churchill studied, Eton or Winchester.

At the age of 18 a few would sit entrance exams for university, but most went straight into a career in the army, church or civil service, with many serving in India and elsewhere in the British Empire. A lucky few inherited land and titles from their fathers and had no need of any career.

The daughters of rich parents received little education.

The vast mass of ordinary children had, since 1870, gone to schools set up and run by local school boards, or committees. Education was provided up to the age of 13, but it was not compulsory until 1880. Few children – boys and girls – who went to these schools had any further education or obtained professional qualifications.

Until well into the 20th century high-quality education in Britain was only available to the sons of rich parents.

▲ Churchill at Harrow in 1890. From there he went to the Royal Military Academy, Sandhurst – following the military tradition of his ancestor, the 1st Duke of Marlborough.

Life with his parents

Churchill's relationship with his parents was uneasy. He rarely saw his father, and seldom spoke to him. In the late 1930s Winston Churchill spent an evening dining with his son, whom he had named Randolph after his own father, and remarked that: "We have this evening had a longer period of continuous conversation together than the total which I ever had with my father in the course of his life." In 1906 Churchill wrote a very readable biography of his father, and tried to present him in a good

▲ *Blenheim Palace, Oxfordshire, home of the Dukes of Marlborough since it was built in the early 18th century, and birthplace of Winston Churchill in 1874.*

light, but in reality, he did not know his father well.

Churchill was closer to his mother, but in his early autobiography, *My Early Life*, which covers his life up to 1906, he wrote that: "My mother made the same brilliant impression upon my childhood's eye. She shone for me like the Evening Star. I loved her dearly – but at a distance." When he was at school, he wrote to his mother regularly, but his letters are full of requests for more visits from his parents, demands for more attention in the future, and wishes that in the holidays he could come home to his father's house at 48 Charles Street, London, rather than stay with family friends. However, both his devoted childhood nanny, Mrs Everest, and a family friend, the Countess of Wilton, wrote loving letters to him. The countess even signed her letters "Your ever affectionate, deputy mother, Laura Wilton."

School days

On 3 November 1882, aged almost eight, Churchill started at St George's preparatory school, Ascot, some 40 km (25 miles) west of London, a brutal school where the boys were regularly flogged (whipped). After two years he left St George's to be taught at a private school in Brighton, on England's south coast. This was a gentler school but the standard of education was very low. While at Brighton he had a severe attack of pneumonia and almost died.

In January 1888, aged 13, Churchill sat the entrance exams for Harrow School in north London, one of the most famous boys' public schools in Britain, and passed at the first attempt. Churchill was not a gifted student, and did badly in both classics – Latin and Greek – and mathematics. However, he loved history and had a gifted English teacher, Robert Somervell, who taught him how to write and speak good English, a skill in which he excelled throughout his life. He also had an amazing memory, which he demonstrated when he won a major school prize for reciting the 1,200 lines of Macaulay's *Lays of Ancient Rome* without a mistake.

In other respects Churchill was a poor scholar, and spent the last three years of his school days in the army form, which mixed together boys of all ages who were not clever enough to go to university but could get into the army. As a child Churchill had a collection of more than 1,500 lead soldiers, which he arranged in battle lines, and he had become obsessed with military affairs.

Army life

Because of his poor education Churchill twice failed the entrance exams to the Royal Military Academy at Sandhurst. In early 1893 he attended a "crammer" school in London, where he learned enough to pass the exams at the third attempt. In September he started as a cavalry cadet at Sandhurst, graduating eighth in his class of 150 in December 1894. The following February he was commissioned as a second lieutenant in the 4th Hussars, at an annual salary of £150, about £7,500 ($10,500) at today's values. His father had died a month earlier but had left Churchill little money in his will, so he had to look after himself.

Churchill's first military adventure was in Cuba, then part of the Spanish Empire. He visited the island as a civilian in autumn 1895 to observe the fighting between the Spanish army and rebels seeking independence, and spent his 21st birthday under fire, which he found very exciting.

When he returned to Britain in 1896 he was immediately posted to India, where he arrived in October. He spent 19 months in the country, visiting Calcutta and other cities and playing polo. He also took the opportunity to improve his education: he read widely and met as many important people as he could. His only military adventure was as part of an expedition to the wild North-West Frontier Province to put down a rebellion by local Pathan tribesmen. He wrote about his exploits in his first book – *The Story of the Malakand Field Force* – which was published to great acclaim in 1898. He also wrote a novel – *Savrola* – which was serialized in a magazine during 1899 and published in 1900. It was not a success and he wrote no more fiction.

Churchill's next military adventure took place in the Sudan, northern Africa, where an Islamic army had driven out the occupying British forces in 1885. The British started to reoccupy the country during the mid-1890s, and Churchill wanted to be part of the final campaign to reconquer the country. He managed to join the 21st Lancers and took part in the decisive Battle of Omdurman in September 1898. His account of this campaign – *The River War* – was a far more serious work of military history than its autobiographical predecessor. He also sent back a stream of newspaper reports, as he had from Cuba and India. Not only did these give him a steady income to add to his very low military pay, they helped to establish his reputation as a war correspondent and journalist.

▶ *As a junior officer with the 4th Hussars in India in 1896–97, Churchill spent much of his time playing polo.*

Life in Parliament

In 1899 Churchill began a parliamentary career that would, with interruptions, last his entire life.

Churchill's father, Lord Randolph Churchill, and his grandfather, the 7th Duke of Marlborough, had both been Conservative politicians. So it was natural that Churchill would want to follow them into politics. On 21 April 1893, when he was 18, he had sat in the Strangers' Gallery of the House of Commons and heard the prime minister, William Gladstone. Attracted by the drama and history of Parliament, Churchill decided to become an MP. He made his first political speech to members of the Conservative Party in Bath during June 1897, and quickly made a name for himself as a potential MP.

He soon got the chance to stand for election. The town of Oldham in Lancashire had two MPs. In 1899 one of the Conservative MPs died and the other resigned. A double by-election was called for 6 July 1899 and Churchill fought one of the seats. But the Conservative government was unpopular and Churchill and his running mate lost to two Liberal Party candidates.

South Africa

In October 1899 war broke out in South Africa between the British, who ruled the Cape Colony and Natal, and the Orange Free State and Transvaal, the two independent Boer republics, which feared for their freedom as Britain expanded its empire in southern Africa. Churchill was still a serving military officer, but agreed with the *Morning Post* newspaper to cover the war as a journalist. He arrived in South Africa in late October and by mid-November was on board an armoured train heading north through Natal towards the Boer forces. However, on 15 November Boer forces surrounded the train and although some British soldiers escaped, Churchill was captured and taken to Pretoria, the Transvaal capital.

After 24 days as a prisoner Churchill escaped and, with the aid of a British mine manager, hid in a freight train and travelled for 450 km (280 miles) through

▶ *Churchill, the prospective Conservative candidate for Oldham, before the by-election in 1899. He was defeated by the Liberal Party's candidate.*

hostile Boer territory to safety in the Portuguese colony of Mozambique. By 23 December 1899 he was back in the port of Durban in Natal. Here he was greeted as a hero and news of his escape soon spread around the world. He stayed in South Africa for another six months, fighting as a lieutenant in the South African Light Horse before returning to Britain in July 1900.

The new MP

In September 1900 the Conservative government called a general election. Churchill again fought Oldham as a Conservative candidate and this time he won, as did his party, which formed the new government. Churchill was only 25, but he soon established a reputation as a good political speaker and debater, with a promising career in the Conservative Party and government ahead of him. He made his maiden (debut) speech on 18 February 1901, immediately after a passionate speech from David Lloyd George, a Liberal MP, future prime minister and soon to become a firm friend and ally of Churchill.

However, Churchill remained a Conservative MP for little more than three years. He was a passionate supporter of free trade, that is international trade free of tariffs (duties), and believed that free trade made British industry strong and competitive around the world. Many leading Conservatives, however, wanted to introduce a system of imperial preference, which would keep free trade within the British Empire but impose tariffs on goods from the rest of the world. This change would increase the cost of food, notably bread made from foreign wheat. It would also hurt the Lancashire cotton industry, which relied on free trade to import raw cotton from the USA and export finished cloth around the world as cheaply as possible. Churchill represented a cotton town, whose constituents would be doubly hurt by the introduction of imperial preference.

On 31 May 1904 Churchill made an historic move. He entered the House of Commons, but instead of sitting on the government benches, he literally crossed the floor of the house and sat with the opposition Liberal Party next to his friend Lloyd George. Over the next two years

▶ *Churchill (far right) as a prisoner of the Boers in 1899. However, he soon escaped and sent an exciting account of his ordeal to the* Morning Post.

the Liberals grew stronger, finally forcing the resignation of the Conservative government in December 1905. At the general election held in January 1906 Churchill fought the Manchester North West constituency for his new party. He won by a landslide, as did the Liberal Party nationally, winning 400 seats to 157 for the Conservatives. The newly formed Labour Party won 30 seats.

Junior minister

In the new government led by Prime Minister Henry Campbell-Bannerman, Churchill became Under-Secretary of State for the Colonies, a junior ministerial post outside the cabinet. Here he dealt with the aftermath of the Boer War, won by the British in 1902, and in 1906 successfully introduced self-government within the British Empire for the two defeated Boer republics, including Transvaal where he had been a prisoner seven years before. He made several blunders but impressed most people with his intelligence and good humour. In April 1908 Campbell-Bannerman retired due to ill-health and was succeeded by Herbert Henry Asquith. In the reshuffle of government posts

Churchill was promoted to the cabinet as President of the Board of Trade, succeeding Lloyd George, who became Chancellor of the Exchequer. Churchill was only 33 – he was the youngest cabinet minister since 1866 – and had been a Liberal for only four years.

Conservative and Liberal

When Winston Churchill first entered Parliament in 1900 there were two main political parties in Britain. The Conservative, or Tory, Party represented the landed and professional classes who believed in the maintenance of the British Empire, supported the monarchy and the Anglican Church and were against home rule for Ireland, then part of the United Kingdom.

The Liberal Party represented the industrial and working classes and was more radical in its views. It supported home rule for Ireland, free trade and social reform.

The Labour Representation Committee (renamed the Labour Party in 1906) was formed in 1900 to increase working-class representation in Parliament, but as yet had few MPs.

▶ *A man of principle? In 1904 Churchill left the Conservatives and joined the Liberals because new taxes on cotton imports would harm his constituents.*

The leading Liberal

Winston Churchill was to serve in the Liberal government for seven years, introducing many radical reforms. His period in office, however, was often controversial.

Churchill's move up into the cabinet did not go entirely smoothly. Until 1919 it was a curious requirement of the law that a newly appointed cabinet minister had to resign his seat and seek re-election in his constituency. In most cases this was a formality; the opposition parties did not contest such by-elections. But in Manchester North West both the Conservative and Labour parties put up candidates. On 23 April 1908 Churchill lost his seat by 429 votes. He had suffered because of the unpopularity of the Liberal government, but also because many Conservatives still hated him for defecting from their party. It was an unexpected blow to his political career.

Luckily, he was soon offered another seat, and on 9 May he returned to Parliament as MP for Dundee in Scotland, with a healthy majority.

Love and marriage

When Churchill entered the cabinet he was 33 but still unmarried. However, in March 1908 he had been invited to a dinner party in London where he sat next to Clementine Hozier, the 22-year-old daughter of Lady Blanche Ogilvy, daughter of the 10th Earl of Airlie, and Henry Hozier, a former Brigade of Guards officer and businessman. In later life Clementine became convinced that she was not Hozier's daughter, but it is unclear who her father was. She was tall and beautiful, and very soon Winston fell in love with her. On 11 August he proposed to her and the couple were married on 12 September 1908 at St Margaret's Church, Westminster, where many parliamentary weddings take place. About 1,300 guests attended; Lloyd George signed the register for his friend.

Getting down to work

As President of the Board of Trade
Churchill was responsible for commerce
and industry, national and international
trade, labour relations, merchant shipping
and the railways. It was a curious mixture
of responsibilities but an important one.
In the early years of the 20th century
many working people in Britain were very

▲ *Winston Churchill and his fiancée, Clementine Hozier, soon after their engagement in 1908.*

poor and lived in desperate conditions.
The Liberal government was determined
to tackle these problems, some of which
were the responsibility of Churchill's
department. He set to work with great
enthusiasm, introducing a series of

radical reforms that did much to improve the quality of life for poor people in Britain and to improve trade and commerce, upon which so many jobs and livelihoods depended.

He set up the Port of London Authority, a government body, to run the port of London and make it more competitive with foreign rivals, introduced legislation to deal with sweated (that is, unregulated and underpaid) labour in the textile industry and, in 1909, set up a national network of labour exchanges where unemployed people could find jobs. Above all, he began to work out a system of national insurance against unemployment to be taken out by working people, a proposal that became law as the National Insurance Act in 1911 and which marked the start of the modern British welfare state.

In order to pay for these and other measures – old age pensions were paid by the state for the first time in 1908 – Lloyd George, the Chancellor of the Exchequer, introduced a radical budget, nicknamed the "People's Budget" in April 1909. He proposed to raise income tax and death duties, introduce a super-tax for the rich,

and tax the value of land for the first time. These proposals were accepted by the Liberal-dominated House of Commons but rejected by the Conservative-dominated House of Lords. The House of Lords often rejected Liberal bills (Acts of Parliament before they become law) but had never stopped the progress of the finance bill, which set the national budget for the year. As a result, the prime minister, Asquith, called a general election in January 1910 in order to get national support for the budget.

Home Secretary

Churchill easily held his seat in Dundee and in February was promoted by Asquith to become Home Secretary, the youngest since 1822. The Home Secretary is responsible for law and order, as well as many other affairs, and is one of the most important positions in government. Churchill continued to promote reform measures in his new office, introducing legislation to improve safety in the mines and the working conditions of the 1.5 million shopworkers. He also tackled

▶ *Budget Day, 30 June 1910: Lloyd George, the Chancellor of the Exchequer (left) goes to the House of Commons with Churchill, the Home Secretary.*

the poor state of prisons and introduced measures to reduce the prison population of both children and those imprisoned for non-payment of fines. He steered through the House of Commons legislation on unemployment insurance that he had begun at the Board of Trade, and generally enhanced his reputation as a radical politician who tried to improve social conditions in the country.

In April 1910 the "People's Budget" finally became law, but the government decided to remove once and for all the power of the House of Lords to obstruct government legislation from the House of Commons. This led to a second general election in December and a lengthy constitutional struggle until the Parliament Act limiting the power of the Lords was finally passed in August 1911.

Churchill again held his seat in Dundee, but his reputation as a reformer was now under attack. Women did not have the vote in Britain at this time. Churchill favoured giving some women the vote, but not at the cost of the Liberals losing power. This made his role as Home Secretary difficult, for he was responsible for the policing of suffragette demonstrations and for the treatment of suffragette hunger-strikers in prison. As a result of his views, radical suffragettes began to disrupt his election meetings and attack him verbally whenever they could.

Calling in the troops

Churchill also came under attack for some controversial actions. In November 1910 he authorized the dispatch of troops to reinforce the police in the South Wales coalfield, where a miners' strike had led to violence, rioting and the looting of shops in the town of Tonypandy in the Rhondda valley. The troops remained in the Rhondda for a year, although they were never used against the strikers.

During 1911 he also sent troops and a warship to Liverpool to help police battle striking dockers and ordered troops to occupy all the main railway stations in Manchester, where workers were on strike. Many trade unionists and Labour Party supporters never forgave him for these actions.

▶ *Churchill set up labour exchanges to help the unemployed. He and Prime Minister Asquith visited a labour exchange in south London in 1910.*

In December 1910 two policemen were killed when they discovered a group of immigrants from Latvia, then part of Russia, attempting to rob a jeweller's shop in London's East End. On 2 January 1911 police tracked them down to Sidney Street in nearby Stepney and requested army reinforcements to help capture them. Churchill agreed to the request and went to Sidney Street the next day to see the siege for himself. In this, as in his other actions, Churchill was accused of acting rashly and making a tense situation far more tense.

At sea

In October 1911 Asquith decided he needed a calmer man at the Home Office but was also concerned by the growing naval threat posed by Germany. He therefore appointed Churchill First Lord of the Admiralty in charge of the Royal Navy, a post he had always wanted and one well suited to his energy and ability.

In the early years of the 20th century Germany had built up her navy and soon threatened the supremacy of the Royal Navy. At first Churchill had objected to building new battleships as he preferred to spend the money on social reforms, but

he soon understood the threat Germany posed and became an enthusiastic champion of the navy and its role in defending Britain. He visited every ship and naval base at home and in the Mediterranean to learn about his new job, and vigorously reformed the Admiralty and the navy itself to prepare them for possible war with Germany.

New ships were built, old coal-powered ships were converted to oil in order to increase their speed, guns were upgraded, and pay and conditions for sailors improved. Churchill also recognized the importance of air power, and in July 1914 he set up the Royal Naval Air Service to provide air cover for navy ships and dockyards. In 1918 this was to form part of the new Royal Air Force.

Apart from the navy, the only political issue that concerned Churchill was Ireland. After the two elections in 1910, the Liberal government lost its majority in Parliament and depended on the support of the Irish Nationalist Party to get its legislation through Parliament against Conservative opposition.

▶ *Churchill was a man of great energy. Throughout his career he took every opportunity to get away from his desk, as here at the siege of Sidney Street.*

The mainly Roman Catholic Nationalist Party therefore insisted that the government introduce home rule for Ireland, which they had unsuccessfully demanded for years. Protestant Unionists from the north of Ireland opposed home rule because they feared domination by Roman Catholics and, with support from their Conservative allies, brought Ireland close to civil war. Both sides started to train militia and equip them with guns smuggled in from Germany and other countries, while some members of the British army threatened to mutiny rather than enforce home rule on the Protestant north.

Churchill's father had, famously, fought home rule in 1886 with the phrase "Ulster will fight; Ulster will be right", but his son supported the policy of home rule. In March 1914, as home rule came closer, Churchill ordered naval manoeuvres off the coast of Northern Ireland. Unionists took this as a threat to them and Ireland remained tense until, on 4 August, world events overtook the situation. On that day Britain declared war on Germany, as what later became known as World War One broke out.

World War One

On 28 June 1914 the heir to the Austrian throne, Archduke Franz Ferdinand, was assassinated in Sarajevo, in Austrian-ruled Bosnia. Austria blamed neighbouring Serbia, which claimed Bosnia, and mobilized its forces against Serbia. Russia came to Serbia's aid, Germany supported its ally Austria and France supported its ally Russia. Germany feared that if war broke out it would be invaded from two sides – from Russia in the east and France in the west. It therefore decided to strike first, and attacked France through neutral Belgium.

Britain had always promised to support Belgium's neutrality and declared war on Germany on 4 August 1914. The war lasted more than four years and required the mobilization of the entire workforce of every country involved. By the time peace was declared in November 1918 over 8 million soldiers had lost their lives, a further 21 million had been wounded, and the German, Austrian, Russian and Turkish empires had all collapsed. Britain – allied to France and the USA, which had joined the war in April 1917 – emerged victorious but exhausted.

▶ *Churchill in the summer of 1914 – just before the outbreak of World War One – shown beside the plane in which he had arrived in Plymouth, Devon. He had flying lessons, but was not a success as a pilot.*

In and out of office

From 1915 to 1929, Churchill enjoyed a roller-coaster ride through British politics, both obtaining high office and losing his seat in Parliament.

Churchill's knowledge of military affairs, gained from his service in the army from 1895–1900, and his command of the navy should have made him a dominant figure in the conduct of the war. However, the unexpected loss of some British ships to German torpedo attacks in the early months of the war and the failure of the Royal Navy to defeat its German counterpart at sea caused Churchill embarrasment. Added to these were the German bombardment of towns on the undefended east coast of England and rows between senior members of the Admiralty and navy. All these factors meant that Churchill was soon out of favour.

Gallipoli

In May 1915 Asquith set up a coalition government with the opposition Conservative and Labour parties in order to gain as much support as possible for the war effort. He demoted Churchill to the honorary post of Chancellor of the Duchy of Lancaster. However, Churchill was still a member of the war council – the group of ministers which decided military strategy in the war. This allowed him to continue to promote his favourite idea of landing a large force on the Dardanelles – a narrow strip of Turkish-controlled land at the northern end of the Aegean Sea – in order to capture the Turkish capital of Constantinople, force Turkey out of the war and open up supply routes through the Black Sea to Britain's ally, Russia.

▶ *World War One began in August 1914. Here Churchill, along with other British personnel, visits the front. Such relaxed visits by smartly clad staff officers angered the ordinary soldiers doing the fighting.*

The plan was a bold one, but when the first troops landed in April, they were met with much fiercer Turkish resistance than they anticipated. Further landings failed to break the deadlock, and thousands of soldiers were killed before the allies withdrew the last of their forces in January 1916. Churchill was blamed for the fiasco and accused of poor judgment. On 11 November 1915 he resigned from the government in disgrace.

Fighting for his career

On 18 November Churchill went to France to join the 2nd Battalion, Grenadier Guards. Two months later he commanded the 9th Division, 6th Royal Scots Fusiliers, leading them into battle in the trenches of the Western Front against the German army. His second army career lasted only six months before he returned to active politics in May 1916, this time on the back benches, from where he contributed to a wide range of debates.

In December 1916 dissatisfaction with Asquith's leadership led to his resignation

◀ *ANZAC (Australian and New Zealand Army Corps) troops storm out of their trenches after their hot-weather landings on the beaches at Gallipoli.*

as prime minister and the formation of a new coalition government led by Lloyd George. Churchill hoped to join the new government, but the failure at Gallipoli was too recent and he had to wait until July 1917, when he was appointed Minister of Munitions, a vital job making sure that the army had enough shells, bullets and other supplies to fight the war.

Churchill served in Lloyd George's coalition government until its fall in October 1922, becoming Secretary of State for War and Air in January 1919 and then Colonial Secretary in February 1921. He was an important member of the government and the most senior Liberal after Lloyd George himself in a government dominated by the Conservative Party, but it was not a happy or productive period of his life. The government was faced with many political and economic problems after the war, and while Churchill was his usual energetic self, he had few successes.

As Secretary for War and Air, he became obsessed with the Bolshevik (communist) seizure of power in the Russian Revolution of October 1917, which he feared might lead to world revolution. He supported the use of

British and French troops in Russia to help those fighting against the Bolshevik armies. The British troops were eventually withdrawn in October 1919, but Churchill had gained a reputation as a warmonger at a time when the country desperately wanted to enjoy the benefits of peace. He did, however, quickly demobilize the thousands of troops returning from service on the Western Front, build up the newly formed Royal Air Force and in 1919 continued the flying lessons he had begun while First Lord of the Admiralty before the war. He was eventually forced to stop learning to fly after two crashes.

As Colonial Secretary he acquired responsibility for Ireland. At Easter 1916 Irish republicans had seized the centre of Dublin and declared an Irish Republic. The rising was put down with great force, but in the general election of December 1918 the republican Sinn Féin party won the vast majority of seats in Ireland and set up their own parliament, the Dáil, in January 1919. From then on the Irish Republican Army (IRA) fought a vicious war of independence against the Black and Tans, ex-British soldiers recruited by Churchill while at the War Office to suppress the republican uprising.

In July 1921 Lloyd George arranged a truce with the IRA and both sides edged towards a peace treaty. Churchill became one of the British negotiators. Although he did not play a major role, he got on well with Michael Collins, head of the IRA, and helped the talks succeed in December 1921.

Out of Parliament

In October 1922 Lloyd George's government collapsed when the Conservatives withdrew their support. A general election then took place. Churchill was in hospital undergoing an operation for appendicitis and only arrived in Dundee four days before polling day. Labour voters who had supported him in 1918 disliked his opposition to Russia and voted for a prohibitionist (someone who wants to ban alcohol) candidate, Edwin Scrymgeour, who had first fought the seat against Churchill when he won it at the by-election in 1908. Churchill lost by a huge margin, as did many of his Liberal

▶ *Churchill with General Fayolle (right) in France in 1915, when Churchill was Lieutenant-Colonel in command of the 9th Division, 6th Royal Scots Fusiliers.*

colleagues. The Conservatives formed the government, while the Labour Party became the official opposition. The Liberals came a poor third.

For the first time since 1900 Churchill was out of Parliament with little chance of getting back quickly. Although he fought the general election of December 1923 as a Liberal, failing to win a seat in Leicester, he was drawing closer to the Conservative Party. To Churchill's horror, the Labour Party had formed a minority government in January 1924. He was strongly anti-socialist and believed that the new government would be disastrous for Britain. However, his own Liberal Party was too weak and divided to challenge the growing strength of the Labour Party across the country.

On 19 March 1924 Churchill therefore grabbed the chance to contest a by-election in the Westminster Abbey constituency in the heart of London as an "Independent and Anti-Socialist" candidate with Conservative support. He did not win, but came very close and gained much encouragement from friends and supporters inside the Conservative Party. During the year he addressed many Conservative Party meetings, and in the general election of October 1924 – the third in two years, this time caused by the collapse of the Labour government – he fought the suburban Epping constituency of north-east London as a Constitutionalist with Conservative backing. Churchill won with a huge majority, and was now back in Parliament, this time as part – although not yet a member – of the Conservative Party he had deserted in 1904. It is very rare in British politics for a politician to change parties. It is even rarer to change parties twice, but Churchill argued that he was being quite consistent in that the Liberal views he held in 1904 were now held by the Conservatives in 1924, and that he was being true to his anti-socialist beliefs.

Return to high office

The new Conservative prime minister was Stanley Baldwin, who offered Churchill the important post of Chancellor of the Exchequer in order to gain Liberal support and reassure them that he had no intention of introducing

▶ *Still trying to get back into Parliament, Churchill addresses a by-election rally for the Epping constituency, north-east London, in 1924. He won.*

food tariffs, as he had proposed to do in 1923. Churchill was overjoyed to be back in government and set to work with his usual enthusiasm.

As chancellor, Churchill had a mixed record. He introduced pensions for widows and their children and did much to reduce income and other taxes from the high levels imposed during World War One. However, in April 1925 he also took the crucial decision to return Britain to the gold standard at the pre-war level. Until 1914 the value of the British pound was fixed against other currencies, such as the US dollar, on the basis of its value in gold. This meant that £1 was worth $4.86. Churchill was personally opposed to returning to the pre-war gold standard: he feared that it would make British exports too expensive and thus uncompetitive, thereby harming the economy which was struggling to recover after the war. But he decided to follow the advice of his officials. His fears were proved right when businesses tried to remain competitive by cutting wages and jobs in order to reduce prices. As a result of the decision he took, the British economy performed badly during the 1920s when other major world economies

The General Strike

After Churchill took Britain back onto the gold standard in 1925, British coal became too expensive against its competitors, so mine owners tried to make it cheaper by reducing the wages and increasing the hours worked by the miners. The miners objected to this and went on strike.

In May 1926 a nine-day general strike took place when workers across the country stopped work in support of the coal miners. All newspapers stopped publishing, so Churchill set up and edited the official *British Gazette*, which provided government information and propaganda. By the end of the strike 2,200,000 copies were being printed each day.

Throughout the strike Churchill attracted great hostility from trade unions and workers for his belligerent anti-union speeches and actions. This confirmed his reputation as an anti-socialist warmonger, a reputation he had first gained at Tonypandy in 1910.

were booming, and many people blamed Churchill for the industrial unrest and strikes that broke out in consequence.

▶ *Budget Day, 15 April 1929: Chancellor of the Exchequer Churchill and his wife pose outside Downing Street.*

In the wilderness

In 1929 Churchill was out of office. He was to remain in opposition in the political wilderness until 1939, the longest gap in his career.

In May 1929 Prime Minister Stanley Baldwin called a general election; his government had served the maximum term of five years. Churchill easily held his seat in Epping, but the Conservative government lost power to Labour. Churchill was now in opposition. However, the new government, led by Ramsay MacDonald, did not have a majority of seats in Parliament and had to rely on Liberal support to get its legislation through. Few people expected the government to last long, and Churchill assumed he would soon be back in government.

However, three issues meant that he was to remain on the sidelines of politics for more than a decade, in opposition not just to the governments of the day but also to his own party.

India

The first issue was India. At this time Britain ruled its vast Indian empire, or Raj, through its viceroy and his advisors and gave Indians few powers to govern themselves. In 1928 Prime Minister Baldwin had sent a government commission, headed by the Liberal politician Sir John Simon, to India to examine possible changes to the government and constitution of the country. The Simon Commission reported in June 1930 and recommended that the Indian provinces get local self-government and that elections take place for a new all-India parliament. These proposals formed the basis of the 1935 Government of India Act.

Both the Labour government of Ramsay MacDonald and the Conservative opposition led by Stanley Baldwin supported these proposals. Churchill, however, was opposed to any self-government for India, despite the fact that his only knowledge of India was based on his military service there more

▶ *Churchill leaves his constituency office in Epping in 1929. Although he kept his seat in the general election that year, the Conservatives lost to Labour.*

than 30 years before. He was, however, a passionate supporter of the British Empire and believed that any attempt to give India even limited self-government would lead to the break-up of the empire and the end of British rule in India. He therefore resigned from the opposition front bench on 28 January 1931. He had now placed himself in opposition to his own party leadership and began to wage a lonely campaign against Indian self-government alongside extreme Conservatives who in the past had attacked him for his Liberal views. As a result, his isolation from the mainstream of politics became increasingly obvious.

This isolation intensified in August 1931 when the Labour government of Ramsay MacDonald collapsed as the great economic depression of the 1930s hit the country. A new national government was formed from members of the Labour, Conservative and Liberal parties, with MacDonald as prime minister and Baldwin as his deputy.

Churchill was not asked to join the new government, and continued his lonely opposition to Indian self-government until the Government of India Bill became law in 1935.

The abdication crisis

The second major issue that kept Churchill on the political sidelines was his friendship with Edward, Prince of Wales. In January 1936 Edward's father, George V, died, and Edward became king as Edward VIII. Edward was unmarried but deeply in love with Wallis Simpson, an American divorcée about to divorce for the second time. In November, Edward told Baldwin who had become prime minister again – for the third time – that he intended to marry Wallis Simpson as soon as her divorce was agreed. Baldwin consulted his senior ministers and the prime ministers of the Commonwealth and replied that such a marriage would be unacceptable, since Edward was head of the Anglican Church, which did not recognize divorce.

Churchill wanted to help Edward. On 8 December he made a disastrous speech in the House of Commons in his support but failed to prevent Baldwin forcing Edward to choose between his throne or his future wife. On 11 December Edward abdicated (gave up) the throne in favour

▶ *Churchill's determined opposition to Indian independence ensured that he had few political allies during the early 1930s.*

A STRONG
BRITAIN
MEANS
A WORLD
AT PEACE
VOTE
NATIONAL

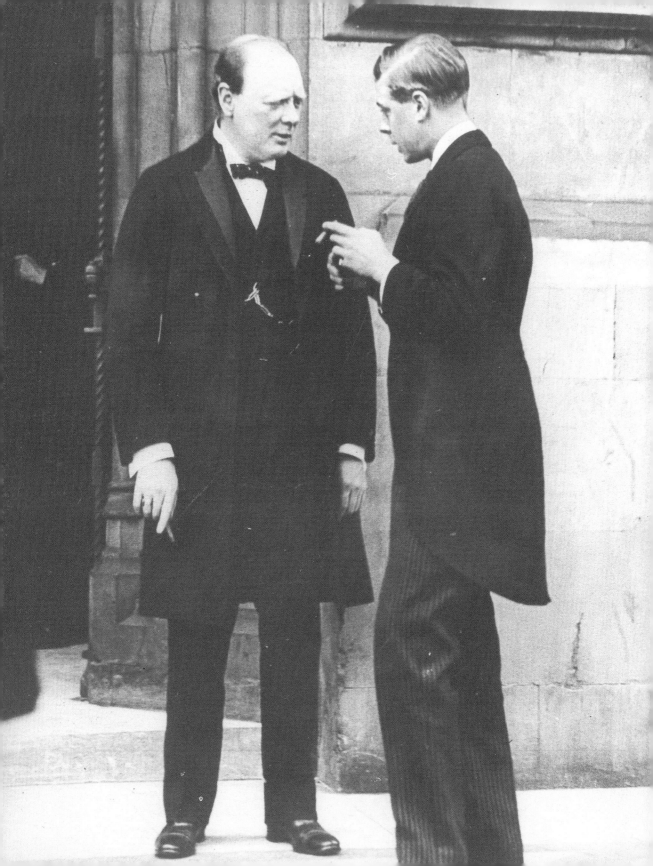

of his brother, George VI, and went into exile in France, where he married Wallis Simpson. The mood of the country was with Baldwin and against Edward, but Churchill had misjudged that mood.

The threat of Germany

In his attitude to India and to the abdication crisis, Churchill had backed the wrong side and lost both times. On the third major issue that kept him on the political sidelines – German re-armament – Churchill was proved right. In January 1933 the Nazi Party of Adolf Hitler came to power in Germany and began a massive programme of rearmament. Hitler's aim was to re-establish German power in Europe and overthrow the 1919 peace settlement of Versailles. The treaty had ended World War One and deprived Germany of much of its former territory and power.

Churchill immediately recognized the threat posed by Hitler to world peace. In April 1933 he spoke in the House of Commons about the "odious" conditions

Many people felt that during the abdication crisis Churchill allowed his friendship with Edward VIII (here seen, right, in 1928 as Prince of Wales) to cloud his political judgement.

inside Germany and the threat of the "persecution and pogrom of Jews" both in Germany itself and in neighbouring countries it was likely to influence or conquer. But his main concern was the growth of German military strength and Britain's failure to match it. In particular he criticized the weakness of the Royal Air Force, which by 1933 was only the fifth strongest in the world, and the lack of air defences against enemy bombers. "The only direct measure of defence upon a great scale," he said in November 1934, "is the certainty of being able to inflict simultaneously upon the enemy as great damage as he can inflict upon ourselves." For that to happen, the RAF would need to be massively strengthened.

Churchill's first speech warning about the German threat was made in March 1933 – barely two months after Hitler had come to power. From then on he delivered many speeches and wrote numerous newspaper articles warning the British people about what was happening in Germany and urging the government to rearm. Many people, however, did not want to hear what he had to say. World War One had ended less than 15 years before Hitler came to power, and Britain was in no mood to fight another European war, especially one likely to be more deadly than its predecessor. The government, with the overwhelming support of most people, put its faith in the League of Nations, an international organization similar to today's United Nations, which tried to tie the nations of the world into collective security through gradual disarmament and peaceful resolution of their disputes. In addition, the government did not want to spend taxpayers' money on new arms and equipment when the economy was so weak and millions were out of work.

Churchill received help in his rearmament campaign from three people. Professor Lindemann, a scientist and administrator at Oxford University, supplied Churchill with much of the scientific and technical knowledge he needed to argue his case. Desmond Morton, head of the Industrial Intelligence Centre, a government committee which monitored German rearmament, and Ralph Wigram, a Foreign Office official, both leaked official information to him so that he was kept fully informed about all the latest government plans.

The slide towards war

In the mid-1930s political events in Europe began to prove Churchill right. Germany sent troops into the previously demilitarized Rhineland in 1936 and united with Austria in 1938, both acts forbidden by the 1919 Treaty of Versailles. Italy, Germany's ally, invaded the African nation of Ethiopia in 1935, while both Germany and Italy helped the rebel Nationalist forces of General Franco in the Spanish Civil War, which began in 1936. Across Europe, Nazi and Fascist governments gained strength while Britain and France reluctantly began to rearm and re-equip their armed forces.

In May 1937 Stanley Baldwin resigned as prime minister and was succeeded by Neville Chamberlain. Once again, Churchill was not included in the government. Chamberlain was a firm believer in appeasement, that is agreeing to some of the territorial and military demands made by Hitler in order to keep the peace in Europe.

▶ *British Prime Minister Chamberlain (left) meets with Adolf Hitler in Munich, September 1938. Chamberlain agreed to Hitler's demand that the Sudetenland – part of Czechoslovakia – be annexed (taken over) by Germany.*

Chamberlain's policy was put to the test in the summer of 1938, when Germans living in the border region of the Sudetenland in Czechoslovakia, supported by Hitler, demanded the right to join Nazi Germany. Czechoslovakia objected, but Chamberlain and the leaders of Germany, Italy and France met in the German city of Munich in September 1938 and agreed to transfer the Sudetenland to Germany.

On his return to Britain Chamberlain described the Munich Agreement as bringing "peace for our time". Churchill, however, called the agreement "a defeat without war". "This is only the beginning of the reckoning," he said. "This is only the first sip, the first foretaste of a bitter cup which will be proffered to us year by year unless, by a supreme recovery of moral health and martial vigour, we rise again and take our stand for freedom as in the olden times." Churchill was right: less than six months later Nazi Germany invaded the rest of Czechoslovakia, breaking the Munich Agreement. War in Europe now seemed inevitable, but Britain was unprepared.

▶ *"Peace for our time." Prime Minister Chamberlain waves the text of the Munich Agreement as he steps off an aeroplane and up to waiting microphones in September 1938.*

Away from politics

Winston Churchill was more than just a politician. He had an extensive family, to which he was devoted, wrote best-selling books, painted and even built brick walls.

Churchill married Clementine Hozier in 1908, and the marriage lasted successfully for the whole of his life. They were devoted to each other, with Clementine often giving her husband good advice and exercising a steadying hand on his more rash impulses.

The couple had five children: Diana, born in 1909, Randolph, born in 1911, Sarah, born in 1914, Marigold, who was born in 1918 and died of a diphtheria-like illness in 1922, and Mary, born in 1922. Sarah became an actress, but the other three entered or married into politics when they grew up.

Randolph tried for many years to get into Parliament, but only succeeded in 1940–45. He later became his father's official biographer, although the two of them often had explosive rows. Diana married Duncan Sandys, a Conservative MP who served as a minister under Churchill and his Conservative successors until 1964.

Mary married Christopher Soames, who also became a Conservative MP and minister. In 1979–80 he oversaw the transition of the British rebel colony of Rhodesia from white minority rule to independence as Zimbabwe.

Two grandchildren, Randolph's son Winston and Mary's son Nicholas, were both MPs during the 1970s and 1980s. Nicholas Soames still is.

Homes and incomes

For all his adult life Churchill lived in London, either in official government residences or in homes he leased or bought himself. In 1917 he had purchased Lullenden, a small country home south of London in Kent, as a weekend retreat from political life, but this was not really big enough for him. In 1922 he bought the much larger Chartwell, an old 16th-century manor house set in 300 acres of farmland just 40 km (24 miles) south of London.

▲ *After politics and his family Churchill's great love was Chartwell, his home in Kent, where he especially enjoyed building walls in the garden.*

The house had glorious south-facing views over rural Kent, but it needed a vast amount of work to make it both habitable and suitable for Churchill's needs. He did not move in until 1924 and from then on the house was a constant drain on his finances. Churchill was devoted to Chartwell, and spent a lot of time and money designing and planting its garden, building rockeries, damming streams and creating ponds and waterfalls, as well as building a large swimming pool. He also helped to build two cottages in the grounds and constructed a large brick wall around the kitchen garden. He used the house as a refuge from London life, and as a place to entertain lavishly. Friends and family stayed every weekend, and he often held

large dinner parties for visiting politicians and other people in public life.

When Harold Macmillan, then a young Conservative MP and later prime minister, visited Churchill at Chartwell in April 1939, he was amazed to discover that even though Churchill was out of office, he kept a considerable staff of

▲ Chartwell under snow. *One of Churchill's paintings of his beloved home, where he went to escape the pressures of politics and public life.*

◀ *Churchill paints while on holiday in the south of France in 1933, smoking one of his trademark cigars.*

secretaries and assistants to help him with his speeches, political research and writings. "I shall always have a picture of that spring day and the sense of power and energy, the great flow of action, which came from Churchill," he later wrote. Such a vast staff, as well as the house and lavish lifestyle he lived there, meant that Churchill was always in need of money. Although he came from an aristocratic family, he inherited little and for many years had to support his mother, as well as his own family. Members of Parliament were not paid until 1911

– although he was paid a salary as both a minister and later, as prime minister – so Churchill was forced to write in order to stay solvent.

Throughout his life he kept up a steady stream of newspaper articles and other items of journalism, published in newspapers in Britain and the Commonwealth, the USA and 16 European countries. From 1931–35, he remarked, "I earned my livelihood by dictating articles which had a wide circulation. I lived in fact from hand to mouth." He also wrote numerous books. His first was published in 1898 (see p 12), and he followed that with a stream of political, historical, military and biographical works. His two-volume biography of his father, Lord Randolph Churchill, which was published in 1906, and his four-volume biography of his great ancestor, the 1st Duke of Marlborough, which was published between 1933–38, earned him great praise. However it was his accounts of both World Wars One and Two which attracted the greatest readership and general admiration. A full list of Churchill's books appears in the bibliography on p 105.

The Nobel Prize

In 1953 Winston Churchill received the Nobel Prize for Literature, the world's most important literary prize. He had been considered for the prize as early as 1946, but the Swedish Academy, which awards it, probably decided to let him finish work on his six-volume *History of the Second World War*, the last volume of which he completed in 1953, before making the award.

As well as his works of history and biography, the Academy also praised his oratory as "swift, unerring in its aim and moving in its grandeur. . . . Churchill's eloquence in the fateful hours of freedom and human dignity was heart-stirring. With his great speeches he has, perhaps, himself erected his most enduring monument."

Churchill could not go to Stockholm to receive the prize in person, so he sent Clementine Churchill and his daughter Sarah in his place.

A life of interests

To relax, Churchill read widely, enjoying novels and works of history. He also took up painting in 1915, just after he resigned from the Admiralty in disgrace over the Gallipoli campaign. Soon he became a proficient oil painter of both landscapes and people. One of his friends remarked that it was the only occupation he ever pursued in total silence! He played polo until he was in his mid-50s and in later life enjoyed horseracing and even owned some racehorses, few of which ever won a race. Churchill also enjoyed gambling, winning and losing lots of money in French casinos, and played bezique, a card game, all his life.

Above all he enjoyed a good cigar and a stiff drink, drinking champagne with his lunch and dinner and a brandy in the late evening to keep him awake into the early morning. He was sometimes accused of being drunk, and in 1936 his friend Lord Rothermere, the press baron, offered him £2,000 if he stopped drinking for a year, but he refused, remarking that, "life would not be worth living". Drink stimulated his thoughts and made him entertaining company for the many guests at his dinner table. "I have taken more out of alcohol than alcohol has taken out of me," he said.

Throughout his life, Churchill suffered from an intermittent depression he called his "black dog". This often occurred when his political life was going wrong, but his relentless energy and enthusiasm for life soon got rid of the dog. For above all, Churchill was a supremely self-confident person whose belief in himself and his abilities, his love of power and sense of duty carried him through a tumultuous and adventurous life.

▲ *A sombre Churchill poses in the library at Chartwell in October 1939, a month after Britain's declaration of war against Germany.*

Prime minister at last

At 65, Churchill returned to government as Britain declared war on Germany once again. His greatest challenge was about to begin.

After the German occupation of Czechoslovakia in March 1939, Britain prepared for imminent war against Germany. Rearmament was speeded up, defences readied and preparations put in place to evacuate women and children from cities vulnerable to German air attack. The prime minister, Neville Chamberlain, offered a guarantee to Poland, and later to Greece and Romania, that Britain would come to their aid if Germany invaded them. France did the same, but neither country was ready to form an alliance with the USSR (Soviet Russia), the world's only communist state and the one European country capable of preventing Germany from invading Poland and other central European countries. In August Germany and Russia stunned the world by agreeing the Nazi–Soviet Pact, a non-aggression pact between the two countries that allowed Germany to invade Poland without the Russians retaliating. On 1 September 1939, German forces crossed the Polish border. Two days later Britain and France declared war on Germany. World War Two had begun.

Throughout this countdown to war Churchill had been sitting on the back benches, criticizing Chamberlain and his policies but frustrated that he was not in a position to use his energies on the country's behalf. On the afternoon of Sunday 3 September – hours after the declaration of war – Churchill was returned to government as a member of the war cabinet and First Lord of the Admiralty, the same post he had held during World War One. He was approaching his 65th birthday, and some

▶ *September 1939: Churchill returns to office as First Lord of the Admiralty – a post he had first held in October 1911.*

▲ *Prime Minister Neville Chamberlain (front centre) poses with his war cabinet, November 1939. Churchill stands behind him, to his right.*

people thought he was too old and tired to hold office again. However government, like politics in general, always gave him energy. He threw himself into his new job, writing urgent memos and letters to admirals and others in his department about the navy and to the prime minister and other ministers about the conduct of the war. He visited many naval bases to inspect the navy for himself, and did much to raise morale among the sailors, as well as among his staff in London. His secretary, Kathleen Hill, observed: "When Winston was at the Admiralty the place was buzzing with atmosphere, with electricity. When he was away on tour, it was dead, dead, dead."

The "phoney war"

The first few months of the war are often called the "phoney war", because Britain was largely unaffected by events in Europe. Germany concentrated on the invasion of western Poland, while Russia occupied eastern Poland and the Baltic states and attacked Finland. For many people in Britain the war seemed unreal. All that changed in April–May 1940. On 9 April German forces invaded Denmark and Norway and soon occupied both countries, despite battles with the British Royal Navy off the Norwegian coast. British and French troops landed in central and northern Norway, but were quickly withdrawn when they failed to stop the German advance. By early May, most of Norway was in German hands.

As First Lord of the Admiralty Churchill bore some responsibility for the failure of the Royal Navy to prevent the occupation of Norway. On 7–8 May, the House of Commons met to debate the disaster. Chamberlain had always had the support of the vast majority of

Conservative MPs, but this time they turned against him and his leadership. Leo Amery MP quoted from the 17th-century English republican leader Oliver Cromwell, saying to Chamberlain: "You have sat too long here for any good you have been doing. Depart, I say, and let us have done with you. In the name of God, go." Other Conservatives joined in the attack in the government, as did Lloyd George, prime minister when Britain was last at war. He said that "the prime minister should give an example of sacrifice because there is nothing which can contribute more to victory in this war than that he should sacrifice the seals of office". When Churchill tried to take some of the blame, Lloyd George replied that he "must not allow himself to be converted into an air-raid shelter to keep the splinters from hitting his colleagues". Chamberlain appealed for the support of his friends, but this time his friends deserted him, and his usual majority of 213 votes over the opposition parties fell to just 81.

A change of leader

The day after the debate, 9 May, Chamberlain met Churchill and the

Foreign Secretary, Lord Halifax. He realized that he could not continue as prime minister and hoped that Halifax would succeed him. However Halifax was closely associated with Chamberlain's policies and, crucially, was a member of the House of Lords, not the House of Commons. He therefore ruled himself out as a possible prime minister and supported Churchill.

Chamberlain then met Clement Attlee and Arthur Greenwood, leader and deputy leader of the opposition Labour Party, who made it clear that the Labour Party would serve in a coalition with the Conservatives but only under a different leader. Shortly after 5 p.m. on Friday 10 May, Chamberlain went to Buckingham Palace to see the king, George VI, and resigned as prime minister. The king then summoned Churchill and, by 6 p.m., had asked him to form the new government.

Prime minister at last

Forty years after he had first entered the House of Commons, and at the age of 65, Churchill was prime minister. Churchill now took up residence in 10 Downing Street, the official home of the prime minister in London.

Although in retrospect it seems that Churchill was destined to become prime minister in 1940, he was not the obvious choice. He was old – one of the oldest people ever to have become prime minister. He led no political party, as Neville Chamberlain was to remain leader of the Conservative Party until Churchill took over on 9 October 1940. He did not have the support of George VI – who resented his support for his brother Edward VIII during the abdication crisis of 1936 – nor of many in government or the civil service. He didn't have the support of most Conservative MPs, who disliked his attacks on Chamberlain, or of many Labour MPs, who remembered his record in office during the General Strike and at other times.

But as a public figure he had huge support among ordinary people, who admired his bravery and eloquence. They also remembered that he – almost alone– had warned them since early in 1933 of the threat from Germany that Britain and Europe were now experiencing in the war.

A formidable task

The task Churchill faced was immense. On the same day as he became prime

minister, German forces invaded the Netherlands, Belgium and Luxembourg and prepared to sweep into France and invade Britain. At its hour of greatest danger, Britain placed its future in the hands of a remarkable man.

▲ *London, 19 April, 1940: Churchill, as First Lord of the Admiralty, addresses sailors on Horse Guards Parade. A few weeks later he would become prime minister.*

61

Inspiring the nation

In the early years of the war, when the danger to Britain was at its greatest, Churchill provided inspired leadership to the entire nation.

Churchill moved fast to create a new government. He set up a war cabinet of five people, including Attlee and Greenwood from the Labour Party, with Attlee serving as his deputy leader. Chamberlain was kept on, although he soon became ill and died in November 1940. Talented people from all political parties, and from outside Parliament, were brought into government to run the country during this time of crisis.

"Blood, toil, tears and sweat"

On Monday 13 May 1940 Churchill confronted the House of Commons for the first time as prime minister. His predecessor, Chamberlain, was given a huge cheer by Conservative MPs when he entered the chamber, but Churchill was met with little support from the Conservatives and only slight cheers from the Labour and Liberal benches. He made a short statement setting out his aims: "I would say to the House, as I said to those who have joined this government, that I have nothing to offer but blood, toil, tears and sweat. We have before us an ordeal of the most grievous kind. . . . You ask, what is our policy? I will say: it is to wage war, by sea, land and air, with all our might and with all the strength that God can give us: to wage war against a monstrous tyranny . . . that is our policy. You ask, what is our aim? I can answer in one word: it is victory, victory at all costs, victory in spite of all terror, victory, however long and hard the road may be; for without victory, there is no survival."

Not everyone agreed with this aim. Some members of the government,

▶ *Churchill broadcasting to the nation. His speeches were decisive in keeping up morale during the war.*

▲ *A cartoon published in 1940 showing Churchill leading his government and the people of Britain.*

notably Foreign Secretary Lord Halifax, believed that a negotiated peace with Hitler that gave Germany dominance of Europe while Britain kept her empire was the sensible option. However, Churchill believed in a free Europe and would not consider any talk of peace. He had to work hard to win the support of some ministers and MPs, but had already won the hearts and minds of the British people. His fighting words, and the many more he was to utter during the war, did much to lift British morale and stiffen people's resolve to fight against Nazi Germany.

Within days, Churchill's own resolve was tested to its limits. On 23 May German forces broke through French lines and headed towards the English Channel, cutting off British, French and Belgian troops at Dunkirk. Their only hope was to escape by boat back to Britain, leaving all their weapons behind.

Between 27 May and 4 June, an armada of little ships, some as small as 4 m (14 ft) long, sailed across from England to pick up more than 335,000 soldiers from the Dunkirk beaches and carry them out to naval craft waiting in deeper waters. It was a both a disaster and a miracle, but worse was to come. On 10 June Italy entered the war on the German side and on 14 June the German army entered Paris, the French capital. Churchill proposed that Britain and France unite as one country to defeat the Germans, but on 17 June France collapsed. Just five days later the French government signed an armistice with the Nazis. This handed the north of France – and all the coastline facing Britain – over to German control. A government sympathetic to the Nazis controlled the south of France from a new capital at Vichy.

"Their finest hour"

On 18 June 1940 Churchill faced the House of Commons once again. With defeat and disaster all around him, he had to be strong. "The battle of France is over. I expect that the battle of Britain is about to begin. Upon this battle depends the survival of Christian civilization. . . .

The whole fury and might of the enemy must very soon be turned on us. Hitler knows that he will have to break us in this island or lose the war. If we can stand up to him all Europe may be free, and the life of the world will move forward into broad, sunlit uplands; but if we fail, then the whole world . . . will sink into the abyss of a new dark age. . . . Let us therefore brace ourselves to our duty and so bear ourselves that if the British Commonwealth and Empire lasts for a thousand years, men will still say, 'This was their finest hour'."

One month later, on 10 July, the first German bombers began to attack British ports. The Battle of Britain had begun. While the fighters of the German *Luftwaffe* (air force) fought the RAF for control of the skies, its bombers attacked Britain's ports and then its airfields. Their aim was to disable them so that Germany could launch a huge naval invasion – Operation Sea Lion – across the English Channel. The 700 Hurricane and Spitfire fighters of the Royal Air Force were hugely outnumbered by the Luftwaffe's 1,400 bombers and 1,020 fighters. Churchill ordered the Minister of Aircraft Production, the newspaper

owner Lord Beaverbrook, to step up production as fast as possible in order to get new planes into the air. As their numbers increased, the RAF gradually took control of the skies. On 15 August they shot down 75 German planes, while losing only 34 aeroplanes themselves. By the end of October the Battle of Britain was won and the threat of invasion was over. "Never in the field of human conflict was so much owed by so many to so few," said Churchill about the RAF pilots.

In late August a new threat emerged as German bombers began to attack London and, later on, other cities in what became known as the Blitz. Night after night, death and destruction rained down on the capital. Churchill regularly visited the worst affected areas and talked to those who had lost their homes and sometimes their family and friends. He always made use of his trademarks – holding a cigar, wearing a hat and forming a V-sign with two fingers – and when on 8 September he visibly wept at the scene of one attack, a woman cried

◀ *Churchill, now prime minister, inspects the ruins of the House of Commons in May 1941 as the German bombing campaign against Britain takes its toll.*

out, "Look, he really cares!", and the crowd burst into cheers. His speeches were printed in all the newspapers, and his radio broadcasts made his voice and his message familiar in every home and air-raid shelter. Newspaper cartoons depicted him as a British bulldog, or with his sleeves rolled up marching into battle. More than anyone else, Churchill personified the determination of the British people to win the war.

Churchill's workload was enormous. He dealt with all the necessary paperwork of government, as well as speaking regularly in the House of Commons, holding meetings of the war cabinet, seeing numerous officials and military personnel. He visited different parts of the country to inspect the troops and defences – as well as to keep up civilian morale – and generated a stream of questions to his military commanders and government colleagues about the war effort. He asked why tank design kept changing so fast that mass production was impossible, why the Admiralty insisted on perfect ships later rather than good ships now, why more planes were manufactured than ever reached the airfields, and a thousand other questions.

Every aspect of the war – from its military actions and political conduct to its administrative detail – came under his watchful eye. Above all, he surveyed the strategic direction of the war, making sure that he always saw the big picture around the world rather than getting bogged down in short-term, tactical details. Thus in July 1940 he took the difficult decision, shortly after the fall of France, to destroy the French fleet in the Mediterranean rather than let it fall into German hands. He made sure tanks were sent to British-controlled Egypt to guard against a possible attack on that country, which came later in 1941–42. Above all, he kept in close contact with President Roosevelt of the USA, whose country remained neutral at the start of the war.

New allies

After the fall of France in June 1940 Britain had fought on alone, with only the support of Commonwealth nations such as Canada, Australia and New Zealand. In March 1941 German and Italian troops under General Rommel began to force the British out of Italian-controlled Libya in North Africa, which the British had only just occupied. In

"We shall never surrender"

On 4 June 1940 Churchill delivered one of his most famous and inspiring speeches to the House of Commons:

"Even though large tracts of Europe . . . have fallen . . . we shall not flag or fail. We shall go on to the end. We shall fight in France, we shall fight on the seas and oceans, we shall fight with growing confidence and growing strength in the air, we shall defend our island, whatever the cost may be. We shall fight on the beaches, we shall fight on the landing grounds, we shall fight in the fields and in the streets, we shall fight in the hills; we shall never surrender."

April German and Italian armies swept through Yugoslavia and into Greece. This led in May to the evacuation of British troops from the island of Crete – the last British troops still fighting in Europe. Meanwhile, the Blitz continued to destroy British ports and cities, while German U-boats sank merchant ships bringing much-needed supplies from across the Atlantic.

The situation looked desperate. However, on 22 June 1941 three million German soldiers invaded the USSR at the start of Operation Barbarossa. Britain now had a large and important ally in the

Churchill and President Roosevelt of the USA on board the US cruiser Augusta *after signing the Atlantic Charter in August 1941.*

war against Germany. On the other side of the Atlantic, President Roosevelt was increasingly sympathetic to the British. In August 1940 the USA had given Britain some warships in return for acquiring air and naval bases in British colonies in the West Indies and Newfoundland. After he had fought and won the November 1940 presidential election, Roosevelt began to move closer to Britain. In January 1941 he sent his special envoy, Harry Hopkins, over to meet Churchill and assess whether Britain could survive or win the war against Hitler. Hopkins told Roosevelt that Churchill was "the directing force behind the strategy and conduct of the war in all its essentials. He has an amazing hold on the British people of all classes and groups". As a result, in March 1941, Roosevelt got the US Congress to pass the Lend-Lease Act, which allowed the president to lend or lease any equipment to a nation "whose defense the president deems vital to the defense of the United States". Arms, warships and other equipment soon flowed across the Atlantic to help Britain.

In August 1941, Churchill met Roosevelt for the first time during the war on board HMS *Prince of Wales* and the US cruiser *Augusta* in Placentia Bay, Newfoundland. The two got on well – Roosevelt told Churchill that "it is fun to be in the same decade as you". Between them they agreed the Atlantic Charter, an eight-point statement of war aims and principles for the post-war world, that was later endorsed by the USSR and other countries at war with Germany and Italy. Four months later, on 7 December, Japanese bombers attacked the US fleet at anchor in Pearl Harbor in the Pacific Ocean. The USA was now at war with Japan, Germany and Italy. The European war had become a world war fought on every continent and ocean of the world.

▶ *An American poster from 1942 shows Churchill as the British bulldog. The USA had entered the war against Germany in December 1941.*

HOLDING THE LINE!

Winning the war

Once the USA and USSR had entered the war during 1941, Britain was no longer fighting alone. However, there were many setbacks before victory was won in 1945.

Over Christmas and New Year 1941–42, Churchill went to the USA to discuss the war with his new partner, President Roosevelt. They issued the declaration of the United Nations, as the Allies were called, which set up the framework for waging war against Germany, Italy and Japan. They agreed that the first allied attack against Germany would be in 1942, in order to clear Nazi troops from North Africa before an invasion of mainland Europe.

While the two leaders planned for eventual victory, the immediate tide of war in the days and months after Pearl Harbor ran heavily against the allies. Japanese armies swept through eastern Asia, taking the British colonies of Hong Kong on Christmas Day 1941 and Malaya in January 1942, as well as the crucial fortress of Singapore on 15 February 1942. By May the USA had lost control of its Philippines colony and the Japanese dominated the whole of eastern Asia from the borders of India east to the islands of the Pacific Ocean, and from northern China south to Indonesia.

In North Africa, German troops under General Rommel took the important port of Tobruk on 21 June – with the capture of 35,000 British troops – and pushed the British Eighth Army back to within 130 km (80 miles) of the Egyptian capital, Cairo. In Russia, German troops continued to advance towards Stalingrad in the south-east and still threatened both Leningrad and the capital, Moscow. A largely Canadian attempt to test the German defences at Dieppe in August 1942 also ended in tragic disaster.

Failures around the world – notably at Singapore and Tobruk – led to rising discontent with Churchill's leadership. On 1–2 July 1942 the House of Commons discussed a motion of "no confidence in

▶ *While in the USA in 1941–42, Churchill was asked to address Congress on the progress of the war. Few foreign statesmen ever receive this honour.*

the central direction of the war". Had Churchill lost the vote, he could have been forced to resign as prime minister. The main complaint against him was that he was both the prime minister and thus political head of the country, as well the Minister of Defence and thus military chief in charge of the war strategy. One MP said that he "wins debate after debate and loses battle after battle". Churchill won the vote of no confidence, but he badly needed a military victory to restore national confidence.

Three victories

In August 1942, Churchill visited Egypt. He made Field Marshal Alexander commander-in-chief of British forces in the Middle East. Churchill also gave the command of the British Eighth Army – then retreating across North Africa before German and Italian armies led by General Rommel – to General Montgomery.

Montgomery was a brilliant military leader who was able to inspire the demoralized Eighth Army after its run of

◀ *Churchill gives his famous V-for-Victory sign in response to an enthusiastic greeting from sailors as he arrives in the USA in 1943 for another round of talks.*

defeats. On 2 September he halted the German advance at El Alamein in northern Egypt, and on 23 October went on the attack. The battle raged for 12 days. Finally on 4 November, Rommel began to retreat westwards. It was the first British victory of the war. Church bells rang out across the country in celebration for the first time since the summer of 1940. On 8 November Operation Torch began as US and British troops landed in Morocco and Tunisia and advanced eastwards. By May 1943, Rommel had surrendered. North Africa was now in Allied hands.

Elsewhere, the US navy had stopped the Japanese advance into south-east Asia at the Battle of the Coral Sea in early May 1942 and then defeated them at the decisive Battle of Midway in June. From then on, the Japanese were on the defensive.

In Russia, the German Sixth Army had captured the strategic city of Stalingrad on the River Volga in September but in turn had been surrounded by the Russian Red Army. After savage fighting in the ruins of the city, the German army surrendered on 2 February 1943 with the loss of 160,000 dead and wounded and more than 100,000 prisoners. From now on, the Red Army was on the attack, pushing the Germans out of Russia and back through eastern Europe towards Berlin, the German capital. By early 1943, the tide of war had turned decisively in favour of the Allies.

In the summer of 1943 the Allies pressed home their advantage. In July the Red Army won a huge victory at Kursk – the biggest tank battle in history – and British and US troops landed on the Italian island of Sicily. Mussolini, the Italian dictator, was overthrown and in September, the new Italian government signed an armistice and pulled out of the war. Meanwhile, allied planes stepped up bombing raids against German cities.

Throughout the year Churchill kept up an exhausting schedule of international travel, meeting Roosevelt in Casablanca, Morocco, in January, in Washington in May and then in Quebec, Canada, in August. Here Britain and the USA agreed an overall strategy: to defeat Germany first and then deal with Japan. Finally, Churchill went to Teheran in November for the first three-power meeting with Roosevelt and Soviet leader Joseph Stalin.

Such journeys were very stressful and tiring for Churchill, who was by now 68 and not always in good health. He often had to fly in a bomber, which was both uncomfortable and noisy, rather than in a more luxurious flying-boat, and was often in the air for almost a day, as aircraft were much slower then. Above all, there was always the danger that his plane would be brought down by enemy action. Such international trips also kept him away from Britain for long periods of time.

Invasion

The first few months of 1944 were spent planning for Operation Overlord – the invasion of France and the eventual defeat of Germany. Vast numbers of men and masses of equipment were collected in southern England ready to take across the Channel. The actual landings on the Normandy beaches took place on 6 June – D-Day – and Churchill wanted to be "among the first on the bridgehead". He would not be dissuaded by anyone until George VI wrote to him asking whether "it is fair that you should do exactly what

▶ *August 1944: the tide had turned in the Allies' favour, but the Germans still resisted, especially in Italy, where Churchill is seen here with allied troops.*

I should have liked to do myself?" After the landings proved successful, Churchill visited the troops in France on 12 June and then again in late July. As ever, he was anxious to be where the action was and not stuck behind a desk in London.

Although the war was going well, there were disagreements between the allied leaders about strategy and the eventual peace settlement. The Americans wanted to invade southern France to link up with the D-Day invasion forces in the north, while Churchill wanted to keep all the troops in Italy to push north into Austria and capture Vienna. The Americans won this debate. They invaded southern France in August, days before Paris was liberated from German occupation.

More worryingly, disputes arose between the USSR and its two allies about the future of eastern Europe. The Soviet Union wanted to move its boundary west into Poland and install communist governments in east European countries. Churchill wanted Poland to keep its existing borders and supported its pre-war democratic government, but was forced to accept Stalin's terms for new borders and a communist government. He also agreed to allow the USSR a free hand in eastern Europe provided the Soviets did not intervene in the civil war which had erupted between communist guerrilla forces and those loyal to the Greek king in newly liberated Greece.

Victory at last

In February 1945 Churchill, Stalin and Roosevelt met at the Black Sea resort of Yalta. There they agreed to set up the United Nations organization to ensure world peace. They also decided on the post-war partition of Germany between the USA, the USSR, Britain and France. The future borders of Poland were established and Stalin also agreed to bring the USSR into the war against Japan once Germany was defeated. This was the last time the three leaders met; on 12 April 1945 Roosevelt died.

By now victory against Germany was certain. As the Red Army advanced from the east, British and US troops crossed the River Rhine in March and US troops linked up with the Soviets on 25 April. Five days later Hitler committed suicide in Berlin and on 8 May Germany surrendered. The war in Europe was over.

▶ *The allied leaders, Churchill, Roosevelt and Stalin, at Yalta in February 1945. Roosevelt died two months later.*

Out of power

In May 1945 Churchill was the leader of a victorious nation. Two months later, he was out of office, rejected by the British people.

Ever since he became prime minister in May 1940, Churchill had led a coalition government of the Conservative, Labour and Liberal parties. He considered it "the most capable government England has had or is likely to have", and wrote later that "no prime minister could ever have wished for more loyal and steadfast colleagues than I had found in the Labour Party". Churchill wanted to keep the coalition in place until the war against Japan had been won – whenever that might be – but senior members of the Labour Party wanted an election as soon as possible.

Churchill therefore resigned as head of the coalition government on 23 May 1945 and formed a "caretaker" Conservative government until a general election took place on 5 July.

Blundering to defeat

The election campaign was the first in British history to be fought over the radio. Nearly everyone now had a radio set and had got used to listening to it for news and information, as well as for entertainment, during the war. Both the Conservative and Labour parties were allocated ten half-hour election broadcasts each, and Churchill decided to do four of the Conservative broadcasts himself, including the first and last. His first radio speech created a huge controversy, when he said that "no socialist government conducting the entire life and industry of the country could afford to allow free, sharp or violently worded expressions of public discontent. They would have to fall back on some sort of Gestapo, no doubt very humanely directed in the first instance. . . . My friends, I must tell you that a socialist policy is abhorrent to the British ideas of freedom." The *Gestapo* was the Nazi's secret police force; to suggest that his former coalition partners in the

▶ *On the campaign trail again – Churchill before the general election in 1945. Although he kept his seat, his government was defeated.*

Labour Party were similar to the Nazis shocked many people. Attlee and the Labour Party seized on this mistake and pointed out that Churchill could now be seen in his true colours, not as a victorious national war leader but as a sectarian and divisive party leader.

Churchill was sure he would be returned to Parliament, as he was unopposed by both the Labour and Liberal parties in his new seat of Woodford (the more Conservative part of his old seat of Epping, which had been split in two because of an increase in population). He was unsure, however, about the overall result of the election, as counting did not take place until 26 July, three weeks after polling day, in order to allow the votes of servicemen to be returned from around the world.

When the results were announced, Churchill and the Conservatives received a huge shock. The party gained only 210 seats and 9.9 million votes, while the Labour Party gained 393 seats and almost 12 million votes. The Liberals – Churchill's old party – came a poor third with only 12 seats. Labour had a majority over all other parties of 146 and formed the new government. It was the third-worst Conservative defeat of the 20th century.

In opposition

Very few people had expected Churchill to lose the election, but in retrospect his defeat was inevitable. The Conservative Party was associated with the economic depression and failures of the 1920s and 1930s, as well as with the now hated policy of appeasement towards Hitler. Everything it stood for was negative and backward-looking, and it seemed ill prepared for the post-war world and its problems.

In contrast the Labour Party had proved itself to be both patriotic and efficient during the war and had a forward-looking programme of economic and social change that addressed the many problems faced by the nation in 1945.

A few people thought they could vote Labour yet still keep Churchill as prime minister, but most people recognized that while Churchill was a great man and a great war leader, he was not a good party leader for peace time. They preferred a Labour government led by Clement Attlee. When Churchill left the prime minister's country residence, Chequers, for the last time in July 1945, he signed his name in the visitors' book and underneath wrote "Finis" – finished.

Churchill was gracious in public about his defeat, but personally he was devastated. He soon left the country for a long summer holiday in Italy and France to recover. When he returned in the autumn he found it difficult to settle into a routine. He missed the bustle of government and found his duties as leader of the opposition tedious and unrewarding.

As a result, he left much of the day-to-day running of the Conservative Party to his colleagues and let them decide on the new policies the party was going to offer the nation. He was often absent from the House of Commons for months on end and instead took time to write his war memoirs, paint and relax at his home at Chartwell. He travelled abroad frequently, both on holiday and in order to make speeches and visit foreign leaders.

Two speeches

Two speeches in particular caused great interest, and some controversy. He gave the first at Westminster College in Fulton, Missouri, the home state of the new US president, Harry S Truman, on 5 March 1946. Churchill spoke about his fears for the future peace of Europe and the world now that the USSR controlled eastern Europe. "From Stettin in the Baltic to Trieste in the Adriatic, an iron curtain has descended across the continent", he said, and urged Britain and the USA to work closely together to resist the growing Soviet threat. At the time the speech caused great controversy, as it was less than a year after Britain and the USSR had fought as allies against Germany. The Soviet leader, Stalin, accused Churchill of trying to establish an English-speaking supremacy over the whole world. Churchill's warnings led directly to the decision in 1949 by Britain to join with the USA, Canada and eight European nations to form NATO – the North Atlantic Treaty Organization – to defend themselves against Soviet attack.

His second important speech was delivered at Zürich University in Switzerland on 19 September 1946. There he stated his belief that European nations must unite in order to bring peace to the continent. "The first step in the

▲ *The phrase, "iron curtain", first used by Churchill during his speech at Fulton in the USA in 1946, aptly described the division of Europe after World War Two.*

re-creation of the European family must be a partnership between France and Germany. In this way only can France recover the moral leadership of Europe. There can be no revival of Europe without a spiritually great France and a spiritually great Germany." Again, as at Fulton, Churchill's vision proved accurate. In 1949 ten western European nations, including France and Britain (West Germany joined two years later), set up the Council of Europe – a sort of

▶ *The "British Bulldog" of the war years is presented with a real one by a supporter during the general election campaign of 1950.*

European parliament – and in 1957 six nations, including France and West Germany but not Britain, established what became the European Economic Community, or the Common Market.

However, while Churchill favoured European union, he did have his reservations. "Britain is an integral part of Europe," he said in 1949, "and we mean to play our part in the revival of her prosperity and greatness. But Britain cannot be thought of as a single state in isolation. She is the founder and centre of a worldwide empire and commonwealth. We shall never do anything to weaken the ties . . . which unite us with the other members of the British family of nations. . . . For Britain to enter a European Union from which the empire and commonwealth would be excluded would not only be impossible but would, in the eyes of Europe, enormously reduce the value of our participation."

Another election

In February 1950 the Labour government had been in power for almost five years and now faced a general election. Churchill hoped to return to office, but although the Conservative Party had renewed itself in opposition and was now ready for power, the Labour Party had a strong record in government. It had set up the National Health Service and introduced family allowances and national sickness and unemployment insurance. It had nationalized the Bank of England, the coal mines, the railways and other forms of transport, as well as the gas, iron and steel industries. It had also taken Britain into NATO and given independence to India, Pakistan, Ceylon, and Burma. The election result was that the Conservatives gained seats at Labour's expense, but Churchill remained in opposition. The Labour government returned to power with its majority reduced to six seats.

Churchill decided to stay on to fight one more election.

Back in power

He did not have to wait long. Many members of the Labour government had been in power since 1940 and were now tired and old. The new government soon ran out of energy and was ruthlessly attacked by Churchill and his rejuvenated Conservative Party.

On 25 October 1951 Prime Minister

Attlee called another general election. This time Churchill avoided stupid blunders, such as his "Gestapo" speech of 1945, and presented himself as an experienced statesman who could keep Britain at peace. He also offered a clear distinction between the Conservative and Labour parties. "We are for the ladder. Let us all do our best to climb. They are for the queue. Let each wait in his place until his turn comes." If anyone slips off the ladder, "we shall have a good net and the finest social ambulance service in the world".

The "new-look" Churchill worked. Although the Conservative Party got 229,000 votes less than Labour, it benefited from a collapse in the Liberal Party's vote and gained more seats than Labour – 321 to Labour's 295 and the Liberal's six seats. At the age of almost 77, Churchill was back in power again as prime minister for the second time.

The final years

When Churchill became prime minister again in October 1951, he was almost 77 years old and not in the best of health. But he was to remain in office for more than three years, and had many more years to live.

Churchill's new cabinet contained a mixture of his old wartime friends and generals, such as Foreign Secretary Anthony Eden and Minister of Defence Field Marshal Lord Alexander of Tunis. There were also rising political stars, notably Chancellor of the Exchequer Rab Butler and Minister of Housing and Local Government Harold Macmillan, – his pledge was to build 300,000 new houses a year.

As prime minister second-time round, Churchill was not a great success. He rarely bothered to read official documents or deal with paperwork, and spent a considerable amount of time playing bezique with his officials instead of running the government. He treated cabinet meetings as an excuse to deliver personal and historical reminiscences rather than to manage government business. Often he took decisions without cabinet approval.

His government did have some successes, however. At home, the economy continued to improve after the disruption caused by the war, and Macmillan's house-building boom gave new homes to thousands of families. Abroad, the picture was more mixed. Britain did not join the discussions that later led to the formation of the European Economic Community – the Common Market – in 1957, and it became increasingly detached from moves towards European union. Churchill kept up personal relations with the new US president, Dwight D Eisenhower, who as general had led the D-Day landings in 1944, but the reality was that, after the war, the USA and the USSR dominated world affairs between them while Britain counted for less and less.

▶ *Churchill nears retirement. At the Conservative Party conference in October 1954, Foreign Secretary Anthony Eden leads the cheers for Churchill.*

A secret stroke

Throughout his last premiership Churchill's actions seem directed towards one end – holding onto office for as long as possible. His heir apparent, Anthony Eden, was often ill, and there was no other obvious successor. Above all, no one had the courage to tell Churchill to his face that he was too old to continue in office. Most colleagues thought he would resign after the coronation of the new queen, Elizabeth II, in June 1953. Few expected him to continue to April 1955.

On 23 June 1953 Churchill entertained the Italian prime minister, Alcide de Gasperi, at a banquet at 10 Downing Street. After the meal he suffered a severe stroke. His speech became slurred and he could only walk a few steps. However, his illness was kept secret from all but his closest friends. No detailed report was made to the House of Commons nor did one appear in any British newspaper. Chancellor of the Exchequer Rab Butler ran the government without him until Churchill felt able to return to work in August.

In the last year of his premiership, Churchill became obsessed with the threat posed to the peace and safety of

▶ *Churchill walks to St George's Chapel, Windsor, in the procession of Knights of the Garter, an honour bestowed on him by the Queen in April 1953.*

the world by nuclear weapons. He believed that civilization could be destroyed by these new hydrogen bombs, and hoped that Britain could act as a mediator between the USA and the USSR, the two most powerful nuclear countries in the world, in order to preserve world peace. "I feel like an aeroplane at the end of its flight in the dusk, with the petrol running out, in search of a safe landing," he said to Butler in March 1954.

The only interest he had left "was in high-level conversations with the Russians". Stalin, his old wartime ally, had died in March 1953 and Churchill hoped the new leadership would want to meet him. He used this as an excuse to stay in office, but in July 1954 the Soviets refused to meet him.

Resignation at last

On 30 November 1954, Churchill became 80. He was the first prime minister since 1864 to celebrate his 80th birthday in Downing Street. The House of Commons presented him with a

Churchill's honours

After Churchill's general election defeat in July 1945, George VI wanted to award him the Order of the Garter, the most prestigious order of chivalry, to honour him for his role as wartime leader.

Churchill refused, because he did not want to become a knight and have to call himself Sir Winston. He did, however, accept the Order of Merit from the king in 1946, which gave him no title. He was eventually persuaded by Queen Elizabeth II to accept the Order of the Garter in 1953.

On his resignation in April 1955 the queen offered him a dukedom, but Churchill refused, as it would have meant joining the House of Lords and giving up his parliamentary seat in the House of Commons. He thus remained Sir Winston for the rest of his life. His wife, Clementine, became a life peeress in 1965 and so a member of the House of Lords in her own right.

portrait painted by Graham Sutherland, one of the leading modern British painters. Churchill, however, hated it: "I think it is malignant", he said. At the presentation ceremony, he managed to say, with great irony, that "the portrait is a remarkable example of modern art. It certainly combines force and candour," but immediately dumped it in an attic at Chartwell where, a few months later, it was destroyed by Clementine Churchill.

Eventually, on 5 April 1955, Churchill resigned. He had doubts about his successor, Anthony Eden – "I don't believe Anthony can do it", he remarked to a friend – but it was time for him to leave the national stage. He stayed in the House of Commons until 1964, fighting and holding his Woodford seat in both the 1955 and 1959 general elections. However, after his retirement he never spoke in the House again, and rarely voted. He did, however, make a number of political speeches around the country. In May 1956 he went to Aachen in West Germany to receive the prestigious Charlemagne Prize, awarded annually to

◀ *Lady Churchill greets Queen Elizabeth II as she arrives at 10 Downing Street early in 1955. In April Churchill resigned as prime minister.*

those who have promoted the cause of European union. There he spoke about the dangers of union between the pro-western West Germany and the Soviet-dominated East Germany.

In his retirement, Churchill continued to travel, spending months at a time in the south of France in villas borrowed from friends, notably Lord Beaverbrook, the newspaper tycoon. He also enjoyed eight Mediterranean and Caribbean cruises with the Greek shipping millionaire, Aristotle Onassis, on board his palatial yacht, the *Christina*. He wrote books, painted, read and above all entertained his family and political friends.

In June 1962 Churchill fell out of his bed in the Hôtel de Paris in Monte Carlo and broke his hip. He insisted that he wanted to return to England, and so was brought back in an RAF Comet to the Middlesex Hospital in London.

By now he was a very old man. He celebrated his 90th birthday quietly in November 1964 – and on 12 January 1965 he suffered his last and most serious stroke. He died at 28 Hyde Park Gate, his London home, shortly after 8 a.m. on Sunday 24 January 1965, seventy years to the day after his father.

Churchill's legacy

At his death, Churchill was recognized as one of the greatest figures of the 20th century. But what legacy did he leave behind?

After his death on 24 January, Churchill's body lay in state for three days in Westminster Hall, the historic hall of the Houses of Parliament. Hundreds of thousands of people filed past the coffin to pay their respects. For a time, the service chiefs of staff took their turn to stand guard, as a mark of respect to their former leader.

As a rare honour, Churchill was given a state funeral, which took place on Friday 30 January 1965 in St Paul's Cathedral, London. The event was planned, largely by Churchill himself before his death, with military precision. The 3,000 mourners were led by Queen Elizabeth II and included representatives from 110 nations. Many thousands lined the streets of London to watch the funeral, which was broadcast around the world; more than 350 million people watched in Europe alone.

After the funeral the coffin was taken along the Thames to Waterloo Station, from where a special train took it to Churchill's final resting place in the village churchyard of Bladon, just outside the Blenheim estate where he had been born 90 years before.

His legacy

Tributes to Sir Winston Churchill were made by numerous world leaders. The Pope called him "the indefatigable champion of liberty", while President de Gaulle of France, who had sought refuge in Britain when France fell to the Germans in 1940, said that, "In the war drama he was the greatest." But what legacy did he leave and what are the opinions of him now?

Around the world there are numerous streets and buildings named after Churchill. A college at Cambridge University bears his name and a US warship was named after him. A huge eight-volume official biography, part-

▶ *Churchill's death on 24 January 1965 was headline news all around the world. Here are the front covers of* Life *and* Paris Match *with their tributes.*

written by his son Randolph, and its accompanying 16 volumes of papers have been published, as have many other biographies and studies of his life, some written by members of his family and close friends. His speeches have been collected together and published, both as books and as records, tapes and CDs. There are statues of him outside the Houses of Parliament, as well as busts and statues in many other towns and cities around the world. A portrait by Graham Sutherland – a study for the one destroyed by Clementine Churchill – hangs in the National Portrait Gallery in London. Coins and stamps have been minted in his honour. The underground cabinet war rooms, from where Churchill

▶ *Sailors draw the gun carriage bearing Churchill's coffin along the Strand on its way to St Paul's Cathedral for the rare honour of a state funeral.*

▼ *Thousands of people filed past Churchill's coffin as it lay in state in Westminster Hall, in the Houses of Parliament, where he had spent so much of his life.*

ran the government during the Blitz, are open to the public, as is his home at Chartwell. A river and a waterfall in Canada were renamed after him. Even forty years after his death, it is difficult to avoid coming into contact with Churchill in one way or another.

A superman?

Field Marshal Alan Brooke, who became head of the armed services in 1941, said about Churchill then: "God knows where we would be without him, but God knows where we shall go with him!" Fourteen years later, when Churchill finally resigned as prime minister, Brooke said: "I thank God that I was given an opportunity of working alongside such a man, and of having my eyes opened to the fact that occasionally such supermen exist on this earth." His reaction to Churchill was typical of many. People admired his courage and determination, especially as prime minister during the war, but were often unsure about his judgement. Once they got to know the man, or were lucky enough to work

The funeral over, Churchill's coffin is carried down the steps of St Paul's for its journey by river and rail to Bladon, where he is buried in the village churchyard.

alongside him, they realized that he was, indeed, a superman.

The problem with supermen is that they are very rare. The word "Churchillian" is now in the dictionary – defined as Churchill-like in attitude and approach. Many politicians have tried to be Churchillian but few have had his force of personality or could match his powers of oratory. Churchill wrote all his own speeches and used his gravelly voice to deliver them with great effect. His wartime speeches are among the greatest and most inspiring speeches ever delivered in the English language, but he had a knowledge of British history and a sense of occasion few people possess today.

Right and wrong

During his lifetime Churchill was often wrong. He was politically responsible for the failure of the Dardanelles campaign in 1915, economically wrong to put Britain back on the gold standard in 1925, internationally wrong in his opposition to increased Indian independence during the 1930s, and personally wrong in his support of Edward VIII during the abdication crisis of 1936.

But he was right as a Liberal cabinet minister before World War One to support social reform, and right to warn the country of the dangers of German rearmament after 1933.

Most importantly, however, when the time came, he was exactly the right person to become prime minister in 1940. Other politicians could have done the job, but it is doubtful that anyone could have inspired Britain and the rest of occupied Europe in the way that Churchill did. Roy Jenkins, a recent biographer of Churchill, said after the attack on the World Trade Center in New York in September 2001, when many people praised Mayor Rudolph Giuliani for his actions: "What Giuliani succeeded in doing is what Churchill succeeded in doing in the dreadful summer of 1940. He managed to create an illusion that we were bound to win." In 1940 Britain faced defeat at the hands of Nazi Germany, but Churchill made the British people believe that they could win, against all odds. Five years later, they proved him right.

In practical terms, Churchill's legacy is mainly felt in international affairs. Churchill was a committed European, and his dream of European unity is now taking shape in a very real way, although probably in a very different form to what he intended. He was also a great admirer of the USA – his mother was American, after all – and it was his warning at Fulton, Missouri, in 1946 about an iron curtain descending across Europe that contributed to the formation of NATO in 1949. The US involvement in NATO helped maintain peace in Europe until the end of communism and the lifting of the iron curtain in 1989–90.

Churchill's main legacy, however, is that he saved Britain from defeat in 1940 and led the Allies to victory in 1945, defeating one of the most brutal regimes the world has ever seen. He led the fight against the Nazis and made sure that freedom and democracy won over tyranny. Without Churchill, the history of Britain, Europe and, in fact, the world for much of the 20th century would have been very different.

▶ *A commanding presence in Parliament Square, Churchill's statue stands opposite the House of Commons, which he dominated for so many years.*

Glossary

Aristocrat Member of the British upper class who has a title, such as a duke or a countess.

Armistice Ceasefire signed between two opponents in order to discuss peace terms.

Autobiography Account of a person's life written by that person.

Back-benchers MPs who are not government ministers or leading members of the Opposition sit on the back benches of the House of Commons and are known as back-benchers; ministers and opposition leaders sit facing each other on the front benches.

Biography Account of a person's life written by someone else.

By-election Parliamentary election held during the lifetime of a Parliament to fill a vacant seat.

Candidate Person who stands for election to political office.

Chancellor of the Exchequer Cabinet minister responsible for Britain's finances.

Cabinet The committee of government ministers presided over by the prime minister which runs the country and decides policy. There are usually between 20–25 ministers in the cabinet.

Colony Region or country that is controlled by another country. People who settle in a colony are colonists.

Commons, House of Lower, elected chamber of the two British Houses of Parliament, consisting of about 650 elected members of Parliament (MPs).

Commonwealth, British International organization of former British colonies now independent from British rule which recognize the British monarch as head of the Commonwealth.

communism Belief in a society without different social classes in which everyone is equal and where all property is owned by the people.

Conservative Party Political party founded in the 1830s which strongly supports the monarchy, the established Anglican church and the empire; Churchill was a Conservative MP from 1900–04 and 1924–64 and led the party from 1940–55.

Constituency Town, city or rural area which elects its own MP.

Constitution Written document that lays out the fundamental principles of how a country is to be governed.

Democracy Government by the people or their elected representatives, as in Britain and the USA.

Empire Large number of different countries conquered and ruled by one government or leader; at the end of the 19th century the British Empire was the biggest in world history.

Fascism A political doctrine that believes in authority, strong government, military might and nationalism, as practiced in Italy from 1922–43 and in other European countries. Someone who believes in fascism is called a fascist.

Front benches MPs who are government ministers or leading members of the Opposition sit facing each other on the front benches of the House of Commons; members of their own party without office or position sit on the benches behind them – the back benches.

General election Election of every member of Parliament on the same day.

Home rule Policy of giving self-government to parts of the United Kingdom, notably Ireland.

Hussar Member of a cavalry (mounted horse) regiment.

Labour Party Political party founded in 1900 supporting the interests of organized labour and in favour of nationalization, social reform and other socialist measures.

Landslide Overwhelming election victory.

Liberal Party Political party in favour of individual freedom and social reform, drawing support from radicals, non-conformists and supporters of free trade; Churchill was a Liberal MP from 1904–22.

Lords, House of Upper, hereditary, chamber of the two British Houses of Parliament; its membership consists of aristocrats who pass their hereditary titles down from father to son, bishops, law lords and life peers.

Member of Parliament (MP) Elected politician who sits in the House of Commons.

Nationalist Person who loves his or her own country and is sometimes prepared to fight for it.

Nazi (National Socialist) Party Extreme political party led by Adolf Hitler which controlled Germany from 1933–45; the Nazis believed in the supremacy of the German people and tried to kill all Jews and other peoples, such as Romanies, whom they considered racially or politically inferior.

Neutral A country that does not support either side in a war.

Opposition party Usually the second biggest party in the House of Commons, which is not in power and opposes the government; its leader is known as the Leader of the Opposition.

Parliament In Britain Parliament consists of two houses: the elected House of Commons and the unelected House of Lords; new laws are debated and agreed by Parliament but must be signed by the sovereign before they come into force.

Prime minister Political leader of a country.

Preparatory/private/public school A preparatory school takes fee-paying boys aged 6–7 to prepare them for education at a public (sometimes also called a private) school where they start at the age of 13.

Province Self-governing part of a country, such as an American state.

Raj, the British rule in India.

Seat Parliament constituency held by an MP; it is known as a seat because an MP sits in the House of Commons.

Secretary of State Senior British government minister who sits in the cabinet.

Socialism Social and economic system based on belief in equality and social justice in which means of production, distribution and exchange are owned by the people, usually through the state.

Suffragette Radical campaigner for the right of women to vote, prepared to use force and direct action if necessary to achieve her ends.

Tariff Duty or tax put on imports into a country in order to make them more expensive and less competitive than the same home-produced items.

Unionist Someone who supports the union of the United Kingdom and opposes home rule for Ireland and elsewhere; from 1886–1922 the Conservative Party was generally known as the Conservative and Unionist Party because of its opposition to home rule.

United Kingdom of Great Britain and Ireland Official name of Britain until 1922 when most of Ireland became independent; it was then known as the United Kingdom of Great Britain and Northern Ireland.

USSR Union of the Soviet Socialist Republics, or the Soviet Union, which existed from 1922–91; commonly known as Russia.

Viceroy British governor of India, representing the British monarch and government in the country.
Welfare state National state provision for health, social security, old-age pensions, and unemployment and sickness benefits for the entire population run by the government and paid for by taxation and contributions from wages.

Further reading

Winston S Churchill (8 volumes)
    Randolph Churchill & Martin Gilbert
    Heinemann, London 1966–88
Churchill: A Life
    Martin Gilbert
    Heinemann, London 1991
Churchill
    Roy Jenkins
    Macmillan, London 2001

BOOKS BY WINSTON CHURCHILL
The Story of the Malakand Field Force – 1898 – military history
The River War – 2 volumes – 1899 – military history
Savrola – 1900 – novel
London to Ladysmith via Pretoria – 1900 – autobiography
Ian Hamilton's March – 1900 – autobiography
Lord Randolph Churchill – 2 volumes – 1906 – biography

The People's Rights – 1909 – political pamphlet
The World Crisis – 4 volumes – 1923–27 – world history
The Aftermath – 1929 – world history
My Early Life – 1930 – autobiography
The Eastern Front – 1931 – world history
Thoughts and Adventures – 1932 – essays and reminiscences
Marlborough: His Life and Times – 4 volumes, 1933–38 – biography
Great Contemporaries – 1937 – biographical profiles
Arms and the Covenant – 1938 – political speeches
Step by Step – 1939 – newspaper articles
Painting as a Pastime – 1948 – autobiography
The Second World War – 6 volumes – 1948–54 – world history
A History of the English-Speaking Peoples – 4 volumes – 1956–58 – national history

Timeline

Winston Leonard (handwritten)

1874 30 November Born at Blenheim Palace, Oxfordshire. *Pg6* (handwritten)

1882 3 November Starts at St George's School, Ascot.

1884 Autumn Moves to a preparatory school in Brighton.

1885 1 April Clementine Hozier born in London.

1888 17 April Starts education at Harrow School.

1893 21 April Watches debate in House of Commons.

1893 June Passes entrance exam to the Royal Military College, Sandhurst, at third attempt, and starts as a cavalry cadet on 1 September.

1894 December Graduates eighth out of his class of 150.

1895 24 January Lord Randolph Churchill, Winston's father, dies.

1895 20 February Begins military service with the 4th Hussars.

1895 November Visits Cuba to watch the Spanish army fighting rebel forces.

1896 2 October Arrives in India, where he fights tribesmen in the North-West Frontier Province.

1897 26 June Makes first political speech in Bath.

1898 March Publishes *The Story of the Malakand Field Force*, his first book.

1898 2 September Fights at Battle of Omdurman in the Sudan.

1899 May–Dec *Savrola*, his only novel, is serialized in a British magazine before it is published as a book in both the USA and, in 1900, the UK.

1899 6 July Fights and loses by-election as Conservative candidate in Oldham.

1899 31 October Arrives in South Africa as a war correspondent during the Boer War.

1899 15 November Captured by the Boers but later escapes.

1900 4 July Leaves South Africa.

1900 1 October Elected Conservative MP for Oldham.

1904 31 May Crosses the floor to the Liberals over tariff reform.

1905 13 December Becomes Under Secretary of State for the Colonies in the Liberal government.

1906 4 January Publishes a two-volume biography of his father.

1906 13 January Elected Liberal MP for Manchester North-West.

1908 12 April Becomes President of the Board of Trade.

1908 23 April Loses seat in Manchester.

1908 9 May Returns to Parliament as MP for Dundee.

1908 12 September Marries Clementine Hozier.

1909 Introduces the Trades Board Bill to regulate sweat shops and sets up labour exchanges.

1909 11 July Birth of Diana, Winston's first child; Randolph is born on 28 May 1911, Sarah on 7 October 1914, Marigold in November 1918, and Mary in September 1922.

1910 14 February Becomes Home Secretary after first general election in 1910.

1910 November Sends troops to put down a miners' strike in Tonypandy, South Wales.

1911 3 January Uses troops to end siege at Sidney Street in London.

1911 23 October Appointed First Lord of the Admiralty.

1914 4 August Britain declares war on Germany.

1915 25 May Asquith forms coalition government and Churchill is demoted to Chancellor of the Duchy of Lancaster.

1915 11 November After the Gallipoli disaster, Churchill resigns from the government and fights in France until July 1916.

1917 17 July Returns to government as Minister of Munitions.

1918 11 November World War One ends.

1918 14 December Holds seat in Dundee as a coalition Liberal, that is, a supporter of Lloyd George.

1919 10 January Becomes Secretary of State for War and Air.

1921 13 February Becomes Colonial Secretary.

1922 September Buys Chartwell Manor in Kent.

1922 15 November Loses seat at Dundee in the general election caused by the fall of the coalition government.

1923 6 December Fails to win Leicester West for the Liberals in general election.

1924 19 March Fails to win Westminster Abbey by-election as an Independent and Anti-Socialist candidate.

1924 29 October Returns to Parliament as a Constitutionalist, later Conservative,

MP for Epping and becomes Chancellor of the Exchequer.

1925 28 April Churchill returns the pound to the gold standard.

1926 May Edits the *British Gazette* during the General Strike.

1929 30 May Conservative government loses power in general election.

1931 28 January Resigns from Opposition front bench over India.

1933 March Makes first speeches warning of the dangers of German rearmament.

1936 December Supports Edward VIII in the abdication crisis.

1939 3 September Appointed First Lord of the Admiralty again as war breaks out.

1940 10 May Becomes prime minister.

1940 27 May–4 June Evacuation of troops from Dunkirk.

1940 10 July–31 October Battle of Britain fought over southern England.

1941 12 August Churchill and Roosevelt sign the Atlantic Charter.

1941 22 June German invasion brings USSR into war allied to Britain.

1941 7 December Attack on Pearl Harbor brings USA into war.

1942 23 October–4 November First British victory of the war at El Alamein.

1944 6 June D-Day landings on the Normandy beaches of France.

1945 8 May Victory in Europe Day.

1945 23 May Churchill leads the caretaker Conservative government.

1945 5 July Churchill loses general election to the Labour Party and resigns as prime minister on 26 July.

1946 5 March Delivers "iron curtain" speech in Fulton, Missouri.

1946 19 September Speaks in favour of European union in Zurich.

1950 23 February Just fails to become prime minister again after the general election.

1951 25 October Returns to power as prime minister after the Conservatives win the general election.

1953 24 April Created Knight of the Garter and becomes Sir Winston Churchill.

1953 10 December Wins Nobel Prize for Literature.

1954 30 November Celebrates his 80th birthday in Downing Street.

1955 5 April Retires as prime minister.

1964 July Visits House of Commons for the last time.

1964 30 November Celebrates his 90th birthday.

1965 24 January Dies at his house in London, aged 90.

1965 30 January After lying in state in Westminster Hall, he receives a state funeral in St Paul's Cathedral, London and is buried at Bladon, near Blenheim.

Index

References shown in italic are pictures or maps.